"Trainers"

To Graham,

Knowing we've all been down this well trodden path! Good luck!

Peter

Dedicated to all those in the racing business
who help to prolong the fantasy

Peter Corrigan

ISBN 1 85714 9033

First published in 2001 by Cashel Fine Art,
Skehanagh, Goolds Cross,
Cashel, Co. Tipperary,
Eire.
Tel: 00 353 (0)504 42194
Fax: 00 353 (0)504 42417
e-mail: petercurling@eircom.net
web site: www.petercurling.com

Printed in Italy

THE OWNER

A story of high hopes and broken dreams...
by
PETER CURLING

CASHEL FINE ART

This story starts like many a tale
In a dark hotel saloon;
Where an innocent soul with hard
earned cash
Is persuaded to spend it soon.

He's taken to the Derby Sale,
They go out there in a cab.
But at the end of the day
There's one man who'll pay...
The owner picks up the tab.

They look at all the horses;
He hasn't got a clue,
But his new found friends will tell him
Exactly what to do.

The bidding's fast, they urge him on,
He begins to stall and stammer;

But they nudge his arm, one final bid,
Will catch the falling hammer.

He's escorted over across the yard,
The trainer shakes his hand.
He looks in dismay at the flashy bay
That has cost him fifty grand.

"Don't mind that lump," the farmer says,
"He knocked it on the door.
Here's a tenner for luck
And when he gets to the truck
Will you drop the lad a score!"

The horse departs, the meter starts,
The agents gather round,
Advisers and consultants,
They all deserve their pound.

They smile and wink,
He buys the drink,
They pat him on the back.
Then he takes them out to dinner,
Sure they never had such craic!

"I'll be in touch" the trainer says,
"We'll enter him in September,
But all his family needed time,
He's a big horse you must remember."

The owner smiles, he understands,
Though he doesn't quite get the jargon.
Of course he'll pay the hotel bill,
After all he's got a bargain.

A month goes by and not a word,
The owner lives in hope.
But the first account arrives on time
In a plain brown envelope.

The months go by, the bills roll in,
He gradually comes to his senses.
They never said at Fairyhouse
There'd be additional expenses.

Convital plus, Plusvital con,
Authority to act;
The farrier, the back man,
They all must think I'm cracked.

The trainer is delighted,
He's schooled and jumping well;
But whether he'll win a hurdle...
Only time will tell.

"We'll rough him off,
A summer's grass
Will turn him inside out.
I'll keep him here, the trainer says,
It's better, have no doubt!"

They bring him up in September
But then he knocks a joint;
If they can get him right by Christmas
He'll run in a point-to-point.

In January he gets the virus,
In March his heels are sore.
By April the ground is like the road,
Which really is a bore.

In July the trainer has a plan
They'll give him a quiet run.
"There's a race for him at Laytown,
You'll enjoy it, it's a bit of fun."

The big day dawns, the owner's there
In his very best bib and tucker;
But nobody's told him it's on the beach,
The stupid looking f***er!!

The wiry jockey taps his whip
As the trainer gives instructions.
"I like this horse, don't knock him about,
If you do, there'll be holy ructions!"

The race is run, they cheer them on,
The horses gallop past.
The owner puts his glasses down,
He's finished second last.

"He didn't stay" the jockey says,
"They went a fair old clip;
He hated the ground, he's finished unsound,
And he wants a longer trip!"

"Never mind old boy," the trainer says,
"I'll buy you a stiff drink.
I think it's time we faced the facts
We need to sit down and think.

I'd hate to admit he's a bit of a shit;
There's no point in messing about,
We both of us know the horse is slow
Let's cut our losses and get out.

There's a decent trade in a horse
that's made,
I'm sure he'd make a hunter.
There must be some fool with a
riding school,
I'm certain we'll find a punter.

I'd like to say I'll get him away,
But I tell you if all else fails
We'll fiddle around and get him sound,
And stick him in Goresbridge Sales."

The owner sighs, he shakes his head
It's hard for him not to cry;
But the trainer winks,
Orders two more drinks,
And says with a glint in his eye...

"Never mind old boy, the thing to do
Is to try and find another;
As a matter of fact, I've one in the yard,
He's this one's three parts brother!!"

THE END.

The Irishman   The Englishman   The Frenchman

Boozy!   Crafty

"Lads"